NATURE DETECTIVES

A walk in the city

Jo Waters

Heinemann
LIBRARY

Little Nippers

www.heinemann.co.uk/library
Visit our website to find out more information about **Heinemann Library** books.

To order:
☎ Phone 44 (0) 1865 888066
🖹 Send a fax to 44 (0) 1865 314091
📖 Visit the Heinemann Bookshop at www.heinemann.co.uk/library to browse our catalogue and order online.

First published in Great Britain by Heinemann Library, Halley Court, Jordan Hill, Oxford OX2 8EJ, part of Harcourt Education. Heinemann is a registered trademark of Harcourt Education Ltd.

Editorial: Kathy Peltan and Clare Lewis
Design: Jo Hinton-Malivoire and
   Tinstar Design Ltd (www.tinstar.co.uk)
Picture Research: Maria Joannou and Rebecca Sodergren
Production: Camilla Smith

Originated by Dot Gradations Ltd.
Printed and bound in China by South China Printing Company

13-digit ISBN 978 0 431 17163 0 (hardback)
10 09 08 07 06
10 9 8 7 6 5 4 3 2 1

13-digit ISBN 978 0 431 17168 5 (paperback)
11 10 09 08 07
10 9 8 7 6 5 4 3 2 1

British Library Cataloguing in Publication Data
Waters, Jo
578.7'56
Nature Detectives – A Walk in the City
A full catalogue record for this book is available from the British Library.

Acknowledgements
The Publishers would like to thank the following for permission to reproduce photographs: Alamy Images/Blickwinkle p. 10; Alamy Images/Gardenstock p. 9; Alamy Images/Richard Levine p. 5; Alamy Images/South West Images Scotland p. 7; Corbis/Karen Hunt p. 21; Digital Vision p. 23; Ecoscene p. 20; FLPA/B Borrell Casals p. 19; FLPA/Silvestris Fotoservice p. 11; Getty Images/Photodisc pp. 12, 13; Harcourt Education Ltd/Malcolm Harris pp. 4; Holt Studios pp. 16, 17; Masterfile/J A Kraulis p. 8; Nature Picture Library/Premaphotos p. 18; NHPA/Stephen Dalton p. 22; Photolibrary.com p. 14.

Cover photograph reproduced with permission of Alamy Images.

Our thanks to Annie Davy and Michael Scott for their assistance in the preparation of this book.

Every effort has been made to contact copyright holders of any material reproduced in this book. Any omissions will be rectified in subsequent printings if notice is given to the Publishers.

Contents

See the city

Where are we? We are in the city!

The city is busy and bustling.

5

Flowers

Flowers brighten up the city.

Look in
flowerpots on
windowsills.

Trees

Trees grow in the city too.

They even grow up
through the pavement!

9

Leaves and wings

These trees have
leaves shaped
like hands.

seeds

And amazing
seeds with wings!

Clouds

Look right up at the sky.

What cloud
shapes can
you see?

13

City birds

Pigeons peck for crumbs.

This pigeon has found
some water to drink.

Cracks in the pavement

Down in the pavement,
little weeds grow.

Ants make their home in the cracks.

Woodlice

Woodlice hide in corners.
Can you count them?

They can curl into a ball!

Who's hiding?

This spider is looking for a safe hideaway.

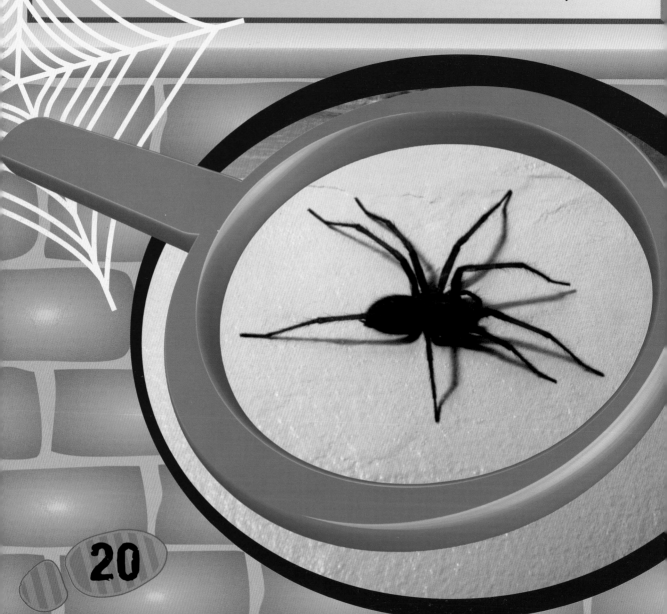

The spider's web glistens and gleams.

21

Evening in the city

As the sun goes down,
moths fly by.

furry feelers

It is getting dark.
Time to go home.

Index

Notes for adults

This series encourages children to explore their environment to gain knowledge and understanding of the things they can see, smell, hear, taste, and feel. The following Early Learning Goals are relevant to the series:

• use the senses to explore and learn about the world around them
• investigate objects and materials by using all of their senses as appropriate
• find out about living things, objects and events they observe
• observe and identify features in the place they live and the natural world
• find out about their environment, and talk about those features they like and dislike.

The following additional information may be of interest
Exploring the natural world at an early age can help promote awareness of the environment and general understanding of life processes. Discussing the seasons with children can be a good way of helping them understand the concepts of time, patterns and change. Identifying features that people share with insects and animals can promote understanding of similarities.

Follow-up activities
• Encourage children to think and talk about why people should take care of the environment and not damage plants or harm animals.
• Ask children about the wildlife they might find in their own garden or home. Get them to think about why some creatures might prefer to live in the city to the countryside.

24